"These poems tell stories of the place where I live and the place I love. These are poems that will touch you and make you think. Many you will read over again."
—Marty Sherman, former editor of *Flyfishing* magazine, and salesman for ClackaCraft Drift Boats

"Norman Maclean wrote that, 'Under the rocks are the words, and some of the words are theirs.' This is the ancestral place from which Scott Starbuck dipped his hands and brought us poetry. This is the human condition diffused like sunlight through water. Starbuck has shown us brightly colored flashes of life that appear and vanish in the blink of an eye like a trout rising then gone."
—David Joy, author of *Where All Light Tends to Go*

"Scott T. Starbuck's *Lost Salmon*, a collection of seventy-nine short poems, also reads like one long poem given the ways in which it accumulates toward a single clear-eyed vision or meditation on time and memory. And which is to say that each moment recorded enacts that lovely-sad mix of elegy and celebration."
—Jack Driscoll, author of *Fishing the Backwash*

"Starbuck is a poet who has fished and is still looking for that perfect fish—and poem. Always happily searching like a good steelheader to the end of the day."
—Frank Amato

"Scott Starbuck has a way of defining the world in these calm and graceful poems capturing the rhythms of water and sky. There is grace and light in his words. A charming collection of poetry you will return to again and again."
—Larry Gavin, author of *Stone & Sky*

LOST SALMON

LOST SALMON

poems by
Scott T. Starbuck

MoonPathPress

Copyright © 2016 Scott T. Starbuck

Poetry
ISBN 978-1-936657-23-0

Cover art: detail ~ *HOOKED*,
mixed media on wood,
by Jennifer Williams.
Used by permission.

Interior art: *SALMON*,
pencil sketch,
by Herb Welch,
(recently found in a "LOST" H. Welch sketchbook).
Used by permission of The Outdoor Sporting Museum.

Design by Tonya Namura using
Gill Sans (display) and Minion Pro (text).

MoonPath Press is dedicated to publishing
the finest poets of the U.S. Pacific Northwest.

MoonPath Press
PO Box 445
Tillamook, OR 97141

MoonPathPress@gmail.com

http://MoonPathPress.com

ACKNOWLEDGMENTS

Grateful acknowledgment is made to the following publications in which these poems first appeared or are forthcoming:

Bathyspheric Review: "18 in Depoe Bay," "Trolling at 6 a.m."

Burden of Light, Poems on Illness and Loss (audio anthology): "Sign"

Canary: "Coyote's Prediction," "Lost in the Woods on Cascade Head" (published under the title "Lost in the Woods")

Cascadia Review: "Fishing Dream Near Yakima, Washington, 7/3/12," "The Other World"

Clerestory: Poems of the Mountain West: "Meditation on Emptiness Between Universes"

CSHS: "Trolling at 6 a.m."

Elohi Gadugi: "800-year-old Western Red Cedar Grove on the North Fork of the Willamette River," "Spawning Run"

Future Cycle Press Anthology: American Society: What Poets See: "Chinese Dream on the Canadian Border"

Hipfish: "Lost in the Woods on Cascade Head" (published under the title "Lost in the Woods")

In this Place (anthology): "Mojo"

The Invisible Bear (Duke University): "Beachcombing"

Local Nomad: "Salamander"

Lost River Review: "The Folks I Surprised in Drift Creek"

Mr. Cogito: "Coyote's Prediction"

Manifest West Series: "Canyon," "Chinese Dream on the Canadian Border," "Truant"

The Moon Magazine: "How Water Moves Past Rock"

Oregon English Journal: "Mr. K's Reel"

Owen Wister Review: "River Watcher"

Portland Review: "True Story, 3rd Person"

Rain Magazine: "Astoria Fragments," "At Barton," "Driving Past Clatskanie Thinking About Raymond Carver," "The Problem With Following Deer Trails When Lost," "September in Astoria," "Tillamook, Greenland"

The Release: "The Fish Who Swallowed Time"

Riven Poetry Journal: "Lost in the Woods on Cascade Head" (published under the title "Lost in the Woods")

Rougarou: "Remembering My Dad Near the Clackamas River in Oregon"

Salt: a Collection of Poetry on the Oregon Coast by Nestucca Spit Press, 2005. "18 in Depoe Bay"

San Diego Reader: "Near Paisley, Oregon"

Scott T. Starbuck's Trees, Fish, and Dreams (blog): "The Fisherman's Wife," "In Old Growth Forest," "July Moon," "Riverspeak," "Spawning Run"

Scythe Literary Journal: "Mojo"

Spillway: "The Tick"

The Steelhead Special: "Sea Burial"

Still Point Arts Quarterly: "Remembering Li Po"

Sunday Oregonian's Northwest Magazine: "Bivisible," "At Rocky Creek" (published under the title "Once, a Red Tide"), "Thanksgiving Lesson"

Through a Distant Lens (anthology): "Back Roads"

Turtle Island Quarterly: "Drifting Out of My Body in the Dark Somewhere Near Astoria, Oregon"

Untitled Country Review: "Local Shaman," "Sign"

Windfall: "In BZ Corner"

Written River: "Forest Silhouettes" (published under the title "Coastal Rain Forest Silhouettes")

Thanks to PLAYA near Summer Lake, Oregon, for a fall 2015 residency that allowed me to finish this book.

"Coyote's Prediction" appeared in the chapbook *The Eyes of Those Who Broke Free* by Pudding House Publications, and *Industrial Oz: Ecopoems* by Fomite Press.

*For Kaige, Lakin, and Sky Starbuck
and all those who come after...*

TABLE OF CONTENTS

I. SPAWN

- 5   Trolling at 6 a.m.
- 6   Truant
- 7   18 in Depoe Bay
- 8   The Fish Who Swallowed Time
- 9   Local Shaman
- 10   Music Teacher's Sailboat
- 11   The Other World
- 12   True Story, 3rd Person
- 13   Driving Past Clatskanie Thinking About Raymond Carver
- 14   Sea Burial
- 15   Dead Reckoning
- 16   At Barton
- 17   Astoria Fragments
- 18   Lost in the Woods on Cascade Head
- 19   Clackamas River Crossing
- 21   Remembering Li Po
- 22   Spawned Salmon
- 23   Inner Space Café
- 24   Tillamook, Greenland
- 25   Underwater Piano and Eagle
- 26   There
- 27   Stripers
- 28   Bivisible
- 29   July Moon
- 30   Riverspeak
- 31   Predawn Late November, Somewhere Near the Snake River

II. LOST SALMON

- 35   Meditation on Emptiness Between Universes
- 36   Back Roads
- 37   September in Astoria

38 Storm Cloud
39 Cliff Salmon
40 Gravity Poem or Three Fishermen
      Discussing Marriage
41 Beachcombing
42 How Water Moves Past Rock
43 Strays
44 Mojo
45 The Folks I Surprised in Drift Creek
46 Fishing Dream Near Yakima, Washington, 7/3/12
47 Snapshots
48 Remembering My Dad Near the Clackamas River
      in Oregon
49 Drifting Out of My Body in the Dark Somewhere
      Near Astoria, Oregon
50 Thanksgiving Lesson
51 Forest Silhouettes
52 What I Saw in the River
53 Sign
54 The Problem Following Deer Trails When Lost
55 At Rocky Creek
60 800-Year-Old Western Red Cedar Grove on
      North Fork of the Willamette River
61 River Watcher
62 The Tick
63 Lost Salmon
64 Sleeping Alone in the Forest Meditation

III. SALMON SPEAK
67 River at 52
68 At 15
69 Barter
70 If Salmon Could Speak
71 Mr. K's Reel
73 The Fisherman's Wife
74 Salmon Telepathy

75 In BZ Corner
76 Pacific Northwest Salmon Bardo
77 Advice to a Student
78 Magic Shirt
79 Poem Celebrating Removal of Elwha Dam
80 Canyon
81 Near Paisley, Oregon
82 Chinese Dream on the Canadian Border
84 Salamander
85 Albino Deer in Snowstorm
86 In Old Growth Forest
87 My River
88 Spawning Run
89 Mirage
90 Pigeon
91 Coyote's Prediction
92 Winter Steelhead
93 Emergence

95 About the Author

"The writers of today, even I, have a tendency to celebrate the destruction of the spirit and god knows it is destroyed often enough. But the beacon thing is that sometimes it is not. [. . . .] It is true that we are weak and sick and ugly and quarrelsome but if that is all we ever were, we would millenniums ago have disappeared from the face of the earth, and a few remnants of fossilized jawbones, a few teeth in strata of limestone would be the only mark our species would have left on the earth."

—John Steinbeck, "The Art of Fiction No. 45,"
The Paris Review

LOST SALMON

I
SPAWN

TROLLING AT 6 A.M.

along a tide rip
with diving gulls,
silver herring flashes,
there is a moment
as the first line is dropped
when dream of salmon
the night before
and muscle of salmon
in aqua light merge.

TRUANT

At 12, I wanted salmon fishing
over Catholic school,

gob of boraxed eggs flung
in silver current

for a giant sea slab
of tugging beet red flesh.

Father Vince said he would make me
a fisher of men

but I chose to be
a fisher of fish.

Once, a police officer stopped
the vet who mentored me.

"Isn't that boy
supposed to be in school?" he asked.

"Well, he is in school," said the vet,
smiling like a drunk cowboy.

"Yes, I guess he is," said the cop.

18 IN DEPOE BAY

My tired arms crusted with salmon blood,
I walked home from docks
hoping to still see a "For Sale" sign
on a rusted out '65 metallic green Mustang
so I could gawk religiously
like it was just off the lot
at a time when I had enough hope
to believe I could save something
from relentless teaching
of saltwater wind.

THE FISH WHO SWALLOWED TIME

I know gravity only works
because of the curvature
of space-time, while

constellations burst and fade
like embers of far away cigarettes
on the Deschutes River.

There was a frog watching a
dragonfly until it lunged
and he was no more.

The moment I hooked the steelhead,
I forgot about everything else.

LOCAL SHAMAN

I tell the diesel mechanic, Bill,
the *Starfisher's* engine is cutting out
due to a hole in a fuel line,
torn flange in pump,
or a shot of bad diesel.

His instructive silence says
my labyrinth mind
must fall through a trap door
to a fishing memory
on the Siletz River

where Coyote,
in his butterfly-colored beads,
laughs like Chaplin
directing *Limelight*
or a man in a rowboat
before there were roads.

MUSIC TEACHER'S SAILBOAT

bound from Oregon to Hawaii
was caught in a storm
and towed.

Once, on the bridge
he showed his left hand
missing two fingers
chewed in hydraulics.

Still, he kept trying,
and I stocked his forecastle
with canned coho
believing like him

in a flawless dream
like Mozart played
over the dark Pacific.

THE OTHER WORLD

Jared buys old fish rods,
not to use
but for stories in them.

"See that bent guide?
It was a monster sturgeon
before the Columbia was dammed."

"Blood-stained cork
is from hand-lining a chinook
away from a seal."

"Date etched 6/4/43
was Gramps praying to St. Helens
and she answered."

I ask "You see all that
in these beat up sticks?"
"Yes," he says plainly

as his railroad cap
in Pacific Northwest wind.

TRUE STORY, 3RD PERSON
—for Dennis

He said, many years ago
his father left two boys
in the Alaskan wilderness

with nothing for food
except a box of Bisquick
and crab ring.

Many nights those boys
listened for footsteps
that never came.

They ate a lot of Bisquick,
a lot of crab,
and a lot of berries.

He said his hunger
taught him to fish.

DRIVING PAST CLATSKANIE THINKING ABOUT RAYMOND CARVER

Rusted trailers and broken engines remain
but so do evergreen shades
and hovering shadows of August coho
just in from the sea.

SEA BURIAL

Clyde said,
Take my ashes
exactly 30 fathoms
off Whale Cove
the second week of July
with tide rips moving in
and immediately after
letting me go
lower green hoochies
and flashers
into the sea,
drag them around
and watch.

DEAD RECKONING

All day muscling in
salmon, lingcod, china rock, sea bass
off the Inn at Spanish Head,
I now stand in Kernville Steak and Seafood House
above the Siletz River
where my charter passenger,
a wrestling coach from Idaho,
confides hard-won wisdom
that "a man's strength
is also his weakness."
I think of all men have lost
to live upon the sea,
my lonely girlfriend gone,
four uncolleged years,
and especially the generosity that sent
Roy Bower and John Chambers to rescue
the fishing vessel *Norwester*
in fog and rough seas, Oct. 4, 1936,
and how men aboard her lived
but both rescuers died.

AT BARTON

At night drowned brothers ask
if I can come out and play.
Their concerns are always the same—
 inner tube, rope, fishing poles.
Their red hair glows like underwater fire
in the green pool.

ASTORIA FRAGMENTS

A few oak leaves remain
as salmon die in the river.

Some boats left
and never returned.

A poster in the Crest Motel
shows 234 local shipwrecks.

On the pier, my blonde leans
into shadow like a mermaid.

Up the hill, baked cinnamon
wafts from Blue Scorcher.

On docks along the Columbia
winter comes late.

Far beyond street lamps, star-berries
fill vacant branches.

Their distant light makes
dead ones shine as much as the living.

LOST IN THE WOODS ON CASCADE HEAD

I kneel in creek bottom
of an alder thicket
to drink cool water
and reflect on how
I got into this mess
merely by following deer
as dark approached.

Last night it was 28 degrees
and I am wet,
soaked clear through.
Glasses lost to a branch,
I laugh and think
that I, the outdoorsman,
may die tonight

and how, whether I do or not,
blurred stars
look like Christmas lights
in giant Sitkas.

CLACKAMAS RIVER CROSSING

Five men already drowned in the river this year,
perhaps seduced by morning mist
or sun's rays dancing on clear water
but my giant steelhead is stuck behind a rock on the far shore

so I wade halfway across a roaring tailout
testing waist-deep current with alder branch
while steelblue flash tugs my arm oceanward
and I pray my hook will hold.

At my feet are red crayfish claws, brightly-colored cork balls,
and snagged silver spinners and spoons alongside glowing
    white bones
of last fall's chinook, steelhead, and coho
that escaped anglers and seals.

Slipping, I think of Portugese fishermen risking their lives
    for cod
and crabbers at Dutch Harbor braving winter swell.
I recall a Mexican drug lord apprehended while trolling
    off Baja
and how it wasn't reported if he caught any fish.

Three quarters across, current pounds my chest.
I think of my angler's life vest hanging in garage,
how I paused in morning darkness
before I left it behind.

I imagine myself on the bottom of the pool
with throbbing rod in icy grip
but, luckily, I climb up three well-placed stones
just before steelhead leaps free,

line goes limp
and I notice river has washed off
winter's mold from my chest waders.

REMEMBERING LI PO

How wonderful in late summer to waste time
making a driftwood horse mask on a wild river
that maybe only I, blue herons, and eagles will see.
"Is that a pear you're making?" asks a hidden fisherman
emerging from alders, "Or maybe a nose?"
I tell him "Yes, it's a pear nose."

then return to carving like it's the most healing
thing in the world, which it is.

SPAWNED SALMON

River stones once loved you
and now you die
with others in your group
perhaps recalling herring feasts,
narrow escapes from orcas,
how even this clichéd moonlight
is so beautiful.

INNER SPACE CAFÉ

"Did your people really nuke men, women, children
on playgrounds and out fishing?"

"I wasn't directly involved."

"Do you pay taxes?"

"Yes."

"You were directly involved."

Outside, Portland, Oregon, rain
brings flowering dogwood

and inescapable silence.

TILLAMOOK, GREENLAND

is carved in periwinkle script
on a piece of submerged driftwood
sparking genetic memories
of rainbow knits on angelic women,
whale tail flukes,
and Sisimiut's Crayola-colored houses.

On the way to the steelhead run,
paper on a telephone pole
says a wife is wanted with boat—
"Send photo of boat."

Here at home, below evergreen waterfalls
I've felt this indelible place before
on river days when there was too much joy
and beauty to speak—
a mermaid who writes on driftwood
with periwinkles
like hidden night truths
that make sense
only in dreams and poems.

UNDERWATER PIANO AND EAGLE

Maybe a pioneer wagon dumped it in the lake.
Maybe by a man tired of pleasing a woman.

Crappie and trout hover the keys
searching for nymphs and emergers.

The gap between its music and underwater silence
is the gap of me never telling the girl

I loved in grade school
she wandered in and out of my dreams 40 years.

Still in my heart is the story of an old man
at Deer Island about an eagle

failing to lift a too-big chinook
thrashing in the Columbia.

THERE

Now, what have I ever lost by dying?
                —Rumi

I'm not the first trout
to go over falls
distracted by a caddis

airborne in terror,
gravity pulling me
through misty rainbows

to blue whirl,
splashing alive
and unharmed

on waterpath to sea
feeding and growing
that was not possible

before.

STRIPERS

Hucking Rapalas in tidal flats,
I waited all night for violent strikes,
and when two happened
my hooks flew up
as if from a sub mine.

I was half in this world
and half in dreamland
so my moonless reactions
were slow.

The next morn
I had only finned ghosts
in the 12 foot aluminum,
great fish, like life,
offering nothing

but two missed chances
to take something home.

BIVISIBLE

Tonight
north wind dies
and watery demon tracks
disappear.

I wade silent,
chest deep, casting
a little farther
each time,

stalking
echo-rings
near sweet grasses,
haunting snags,

drifting fly
to crimson slashes
of sea run trout.

JULY MOON

Maybe death is like the day
I floated an Oregon coastal river
so tranced by summer steelhead,
periwinkle cities, and wildflower scents,
I missed the boat ramp,
and discovered
I didn't care
but kept fishing
under warm July moon.

RIVERSPEAK

After two days without speaking,
river speaks below my raft,
and steelhead whisper
they are going
to whack the hell
out of my spinner.

Each day river flowed
beneath sentinel spruce.
I had a real choice
in my mind
to be here or not,
and much too often
I chose wrong.

PREDAWN LATE NOVEMBER, SOMEWHERE NEAR THE SNAKE RIVER

The road down Hell's Canyon is so bad
Molly Hatchet's "Flirtin' With Disaster"
plays in my head in a Möbius strip.

Three guys on bar stools warned
"We're the guys from *Deliverance*
so be careful out there."

While descending, characters dissolve
and new ones arrive—
river, stone, hawk, leaping fish.

Old skins slough like a rattler,
and the residual moon becomes a
hole in the sky to crawl through.

II
LOST SALMON

MEDITATION ON EMPTINESS BETWEEN UNIVERSES

Under night sky by winding creek
my lakeside campfire will burn out,
rest,
and come morning I will light another,

an idea at first
rising from emptiness and ashes,
to tiny roaring orange
and glowing hot coals.

Last night I was in dreamland, but now
under evergreen shade and birdsong
there will be hotcakes
and blueberry tea.

BACK ROADS

A Native woman sent me 10 miles in the wrong direction
until I stood beside my idling gold Camry.
I imagined her roaring laughter
by a wood stove in December

as she spoke about trickster Coyote
and the steelheaded fisherman.
On back roads I saw nets
like lines in human faces

along swollen river
then friendly truthful elders
and boat with raven bow.
Later, I drove south because

sometimes a man is so polluted by life
he needs a river big as the Columbia
to heal him.

SEPTEMBER IN ASTORIA

The chaos of knowing in September
brings heavy responsibility
for celebration

during lavender
and silver-sided coho run before
all is wet in rain and snow.

Evergreens dance.
Stone Water Woman grins up
through crow shadows

in oaky depths.

STORM CLOUD

Oh, unnamable joy, for with you
comes heavy rain, and salmon
in swollen rivers, men laughing
easily and often

telling stories, some true,
patiently cast spinners
like metaphors of hope
shimmering dreams ready and willing

of ancient giants, gorgeous women,
hidden treasure brought to surface.

CLIFF SALMON

Monster chinook bit my lure, my foot slipped,
and I crashed 14 feet into the water with a butt cushioned
by stones.
Stuart jabbed me with a net to save my life but I told him to
    get the fish.

I was a wet version of Sam McGee standing heart-deep,
bloody arms and legs, happily watching the olive-spotted slab
of ocean-bright silver run, roll, head-shake and leap.

Five freight train runs and still strong enough to make the
    reel sing.
Five freight train runs and still strong enough to break from
that other world.

Our adrenaline surged around boulders into slack water,
him eyeing crazy fishermen who wouldn't let go,
me eyeing ancient prize of 10,000 years of wild red flesh,

brought together by hard rain down the mountain,
he, eventually tearing free of the hook, and I, outside the
    flames of time
for only as long as we fought.

GRAVITY POEM OR THREE FISHERMEN DISCUSSING MARRIAGE

The first says when he was a young buck
one of his favorite gals got pregnant
so he did the right thing.

"Should have pushed her down the stairs,"
jokes the second.

The third says he drew a cow elk tag.

This conversation is intolerable
so 5 minutes later the second tells about
the cow elk he shot with a live bull inside.
"Made me so sick it was my last hunt."

"Happened to me too," says the first,
"and Buster asked what was up
with my watery eyes."

Ron, my toughest high school friend, cried
when it happened to him
but I don't say anything.

Far offshore, a troller taking on water
and listing badly
starts bilge pumps and rights her deck.

BEACHCOMBING

Old men wave metal detectors
like hazmat teams
scanning for radiation.

A man speaks to a stuffed parrot
on his shoulder
like it's alive.

A former scientist
wears a football helmet
and pushes a shopping cart.

"Columbo" says one December,
wood planks split
and dover sole clogged bilge pumps

in a boat like these men
that almost sank
but didn't.

HOW WATER MOVES PAST ROCK

is what salmon read to get home.

I consider this as I recall Mike,
a 56-year-old quad in a wheelchair
who could walk if he had been left
until medics arrived,

and Ross, a half-blind Korean War vet
who taught me to troll on the Willamette River.
20 years passed before I learned
he fought at Porkchop Hill,
and carried a man named Tex 12 miles.

Whitewater says with hard things like these,
find whatever and whoever you must hear,
fight, or dance with
to get where you are going,
to give birth, even if you are male,
to a long ago dream of going from Venice Beach
to Venice, Italy,
in your salmon heart.

Once, Shura and I had to leave
the Columbia Gorge Discovery Center early
to make way for a wedding party
and, since five years had passed,
I felt bad my artist lover and I had not yet married,

then, somewhere near Cascade Locks
I knew in ways that mattered most
we already were.

STRAYS

on the Oregon coast are salmon who run up the wrong river
and swim in ditches, cow pastures, even Hwy 101.

Motorists gawk and take photos
while a cameraman films in rain for evening news.

These salmons' ancient sense of smell is gone and with it
any hope of finding evergreen refuge.

After rain stops and waters recede,
many are dead near a highway or ditch

then plowed under and soon forgotten
like boys here who do meth

and girls who love them.

MOJO

I expected heaven was lavender and glaciers.

Instead, I saw cigarette orbs
burned in a kid's arm that healed.

Prostitute turned social worker.

Banker turned farmer.

Here, in the high country,
dogma is more distant than Nepal.

And, for once, in my rusty shed body,
after long burning of conscience
listening to the others,
there is a temple of silence

like when I was 19 and my glasses fell
in a secret river.

I put them back on and saw that river
was forever on my mind.

THE FOLKS I SURPRISED IN DRIFT CREEK

Trout fishing in remote wilderness,
I saw sex—arms and legs in the way
like when these creatures had finned hunger
and nothing else—

no diamond or gold rings to bond them
but only diamond scales and red-gold flanks
wanting only what the current wanted,
to breathe and move freely

elsewhere in Oregon
far beyond aluminum trailers
or well-traveled roads,
or on the spinning blue ball

like countless others
for as long as possible
floating through mind-forests
of now's expanding universe.

FISHING DREAM NEAR YAKIMA, WASHINGTON, 7/3/12

I know a man
who tried to walk on water
but the hem of his robe
was bit by a salmon
so he tumbled head first
over Roza Falls

and you might say
his death was birth
of caddis larva in armpits
and eye sockets.

Yellow irises found roots
where his heart had been
and would never be again.

SNAPSHOTS

Rising nymphs eaten by trout.

Two trout roasted over coals.

Mother's grave
beside one waiting.

After father left,
she sat in the car
reading as I fished,

or doing macramé

while the river took me
with it into the real beyond

as the time at Rose Festival
our Ferris Wheel paused
long enough to see
two fraying bolts holding up
what was left of industrial sky.

REMEMBERING MY DAD NEAR THE CLACKAMAS RIVER IN OREGON

I'm here because my father is dying.

Because I caught my first salmon at River Mill.

Because bones of my favorite border collie
are in a cathedral of sword ferns.

Because I found a rusted bike
tossed from Cazadero Bridge
and imagined stories about it for years.

Because someone put up a rope swing then disappeared.

Because yesterday I put a stepped-on salamander
out of its quivering pain,
and saved another half swallowed by a snake.

Because when I said the river was bathtub warm
and my submerged father discovered it wasn't,
his laugh echoed through Barton's cliffs.

Because I was seven.

Because I had never seen him so happy.

DRIFTING OUT OF MY BODY IN THE DARK SOMEWHERE NEAR ASTORIA, OREGON

Reds and yellows ghost the river bridge
as stars fade and I slowly cast, waiting for a strike.
Under ancient Sitka spruce
a headlamp shows my boots in a net
and this reminds me of the boot owner's
tiny human gill slits
in the womb when all of these salmon
were his brothers and sisters.

When he eats them, they become him
and, like their river fire, his striving
at any cost
to get back home.

THANKSGIVING LESSON

From our canoe
the next bend in the river
shows a boy
with his first steelhead.

"Beautiful," says Gary
about the sleek fish,
red-bearded man,
black and white panting collie,
beaming son.

"Looks like an early winter-run."
Featherlike
our canoe glides
with three chinook tails
hidden in burlap.

Under fiery trees
leaves drift
in silence.

FOREST SILHOUETTES

We could teach the boy what we know about fishing
but it will be more fun, for him and us,
if we watch him in silence.

He will fall through deadwood, scrape face on devil's club,
lose footing on river stones,
eventually land a gasping salmon.

His shout will echo in old growth.
He will eat red flesh with a pleasure he has never known.
He will be a silhouette like us soon enough.

WHAT I SAW IN THE RIVER

may have been a sturgeon,
submarine,
or dead body,

and since it was a dream
the thread of it
connected back to me.

Reality is different.
It doesn't care
who or what I am,

but only if I see
what it sees
in all directions,

worst sinners
morphing one by one
into saints,

Pacific cloud forests
into cities
and back again.

SIGN

Deer carcass,
cougar track.

Blue heron feathers,
coyote track.

Shura's ashes in river,
flowers in stone.

Eagle shadow,
no eagle.

THE PROBLEM FOLLOWING DEER TRAILS WHEN LOST

is they almost never take you
to Burger King.

They can go straight uphill
and straight down.

Deer also like circles,
figure eights and spirals.

They don't care if you get home
by five or February.

AT ROCKY CREEK

I
Just north of Miroco's pastel cottages
and inland of Otter Crest Loop
I follow a worn trail
away from an old logging road
into a hidden gorge
where late afternoon cutthroat trout
slap emerging caddis flies.

Crystal current meanders through fallen logs,
past sun-lit riffles,
fanning across a brown sand delta
of honeysuckle and cattail.
Gone now are Native canoes,
raised totems, cedar huts,
ritual shell middens and potlatches.
Instead, the creek slips through
a graveyard of giant evergreens
and enters an ochre gate
of rusty railroad track
to a concrete tunnel beneath Highway 101.

Above, the man-made wall
casts a shadow on the water
monument to salmon
floating belly-up in crisp Pacific moonlight
many years ago
beneath the spouting concrete culvert
—their ancient way home blocked—
vanishing one by one
like agates dropped into the sea.

I fish the pools in the secluded canyon,
clouds part, and rays of sunlight
strike crystal waters
like rays in Bible pictures
reminding me of days offshore
trolling for silvers along tide rips
where the blocked creek mouth
first caught my attention.

II
I close my eyes and remember
my days on the *Starfisher*.
As the bow slices water
a wide pink veil
lifts from the rocky coastline.

Wooden boats approach
the frantic diving gulls,
fast and furious salmon.
The cry of "Fish on!"
joins the rush
of the summer morning.

Pelicans cruise in formation
just above the surface.
Puffins bob for bait fish.
Albatross soar on the horizon.

Gray Whales migrate north in pairs,
their 12-foot-wide, twin-fluked tails
rise from dark waters.
Forty-foot breaching loners

vault again and again above the surface
like huge hooked rainbow trout.

Orcas chase schools of silvers.

Dorsal fins of blue sharks
slice V-paths in lake-calm waters.
Flat silvery ocean sunfish,
as large as an engine hatch,
bask like creatures from outer space.
Tropical sea turtles lazily paddle
in warm offshore current.

III
Back to the present,
I rest on a mossy boulder,
clip the caddis fly
and tie on a stone fly nymph.

A few remaining
Sitka spruce trees, 150-feet or so tall,
stretch up as if to see over the wall.

Evening wind flows
down from Cape Foulweather
and through the Sitka Spruce,
leaves its tracks on pools
shining in the canyon.

Quietly, it asks me,
"Who erects this barrier
where there should be a bridge?"

In the Pacific Ocean, land and sky
migrations of men
replace the ancient ones of animals.

New condominiums—
Sea Ridge, Thundering Shores,
Little Whale Cove—
change the face of the coast,
crowd pastel cottages
and open spaces along the sea.

Gray concrete pools
in modern salmon ranches
at Yaquina and Coos Bay
substitute for cascading creeks
such as this one, where hook-nosed bucks
and plump hens
once planted the secret life of the race
beneath autumn leaves and pebbles
to burst forth again with spring rains.

It is nearly dark. I stand knee-deep,
roll-cast the nymph
along a bank of submerged logs.
There is a vibration in the rod tip.
I set the hook, ratchet reel,
guide the half-foot fish to shore—
crimson throat slashes,
bright orange black-spotted fins,
olive back and rosy gill plates.
I remove the hook from its lip
and it darts away,

slips quickly
into cover of gnarled roots.

800-YEAR-OLD WESTERN RED CEDAR GROVE ON NORTH FORK OF THE WILLAMETTE RIVER

Some say
we came from nowhere.

Others say
we came from somewhere.

I am from here.

RIVER WATCHER

Sometimes if you watch
long enough
a rock grows fins.

Other times a branch
becomes a deer antler

or an oak hole
the face of an owl.

Once, when I was nine
in the evening woods
my fear of dark changed
to fear of going home.

THE TICK

As I fished, the tick fished
and blood was
the name of the game.

I got mine, and he got his
then we were cruel
to each other

as brothers can be.

LOST SALMON

I can relate, brother,
as I gasp smog,

my ancient Celtic gills
wanting waters

with my own kind
to sing at birth and death

and just be.

SLEEPING ALONE IN THE FOREST MEDITATION

In the sea of stars
away at last
from the illusion
the world is having
about itself

I begin the slow descent
through treacherous canyons
of the unconscious
out to where the trail ends
on a jagged precipice,

wind in my hair,
confused, I backtrack
again, seven times
to find my way
to the source—

morning light and
bees going
from snapdragon
to snapdragon.

III
SALMON SPEAK

RIVER AT 52

I know if I can just get to the river everything will be okay.
The prism current will carry my dead mother, father,
 partner
Shura whose ashes I left here under an eagle sky.

Lost house, dead cat, will fade
as my weighted apricot fly with mallard wing
works her magic in rain-swollen pools.

My jaw tightens as I grade stack after stack after stack
from men and women who don't want to write,
who force themselves into strange unnatural positions

so unlike salmon, steelhead, and men sure where they
 belong
and where they are going misty days and nights
in the V between coastal mountains.

AT 15

a shapely French girl
took my hand
to her room,

after her parents
fell asleep
during a war film,

sat on the edge
of her bed
and offered sex.

"How about
let's pray instead?"
I replied.

I asked God to give her
immeasurable
glowing peace,

to let her know
she was loved
in a way no human could.

I left her then,
slept on the couch,
all night dreamed of salmon.

BARTER

On a rock ledge she says she will trade
3 fears for an insecurity.

"I'd like to," I say, "but I have a storage unit
full of them in Troutdale."

"How about love?" I counter.
"Can't give what I don't have."

An Indian postcard shows where two lovers
forbidden to marry leapt to their deaths.

I drew stick figures of them falling
and made a joke of it

but driving canyon roads home
thinking of blue mayflies rising

I didn't laugh.

IF SALMON COULD SPEAK

in their dock bins
they would say
captains on phones with wives
lied like sleeping dogs
about doing "boat work"
when really they drank beer
and told sea stories.

They would say
they overheard
some fishermen,
like salmon, bit lures
that got them clubbed
by mermaids or bankers
or both.

They would note
it's greed, in the end,
that kills us all
when enough
is never enough
to resist one more
tempting snack
of the belly or mind
or worse.

MR. K'S REEL

Mr. K only casts 6 or 8 feet
while his boys fling spinners 40
in Molalla River pools.

It isn't arthritis.
His wife was told
about the cheap reel

but she was from Kansas
where saving money
was second religion

so words like "trolling"
and "casting"
meant nothing.

It was unforgivable
but Mr. K smiled
with no hope of a fish.

When his son Luke criticized
his mother's gift,
Mr. K said some things

are more important
than fishing
though we couldn't guess what.

I think of Mr. K
when I pause to answer
a youngster's questions

or help a new angler
with gear
or directions, and

I thought of him today
when a newbie
across Secret Creek

stepped over a ledge
where my fish had been,
and was greeted only

with smile and wave.

THE FISHERMAN'S WIFE

I tell her I lost the salmon.

"Did you check your leader
for wind knots?"

I say "Yes, but I was too lazy
to change it."

"Well then, it's your fault
isn't it?"

I'm used to this kind of sympathy.

She is as exacting as the river
and as beautiful.

SALMON TELEPATHY

Here in the river of shadows and blazing light,
once you accept death of your marble mind,

smolt stage and ocean travels,
of your ideas about who Creator is

and what Creator does
for fish, bears, eagles, humans

on this water planet
making all things new

in milt and orange orbs,
you are ready

as your pale body fades
into roots and stones.

IN BZ CORNER

propane tanks hover like mini-submarines
and there is a stuffed skunk from the Kreps boys
mounted with deer and elk at the gas station.

Mt. Adams glaciers feed rivers and trees.

I found bear vertebrae near an antique reel in the river,
and hooked trout arcing like flames.

It was here I recalled Ross's cigarette embers flicked
    nonchalantly
like shooting stars and, as the son of an alcoholic,
how much I needed his fish stories about Columbia
    River salmon
and high mountain brook trout
before the cancer took him home.

PACIFIC NORTHWEST SALMON BARDO

The alevin is the gap
between egg and stream.

The smolt is the gap
between stream and sea.

The adult is the gap
between sea and egg.

Sooner or later
maybe a fish knows

it's all gap.

ADVICE TO A STUDENT

If you want an audience
go into advertising
instead of poetry.
Understand?

In Oregon's Great Basin
the sage sparrow
with it's huge black spot
like a hole in the middle of
its white breast

doesn't wait
for an audience
to sing.

MAGIC SHIRT

In your lucid dreams
walk through granite,
fly in a magic shirt,
breathe underwater
in kelp forests,
swim up waterfalls,
and disrobe
the most beautiful women
in the universe
until, like Faust,
you are weary of games
and wander below
the village bridge
before dark
to remember how
as a boy
you were happier
walking a lab
through a forest,
seeing winter sun
through evergreens,
holding something real
as a planet-shaped agate
in a starry creek.

POEM CELEBRATING REMOVAL OF ELWHA DAM

Upriver spawning redds
have waited for salmon
unable to get home.

Eagles and hawks
have mistaken rock shadows
for fish.

Soon silver-blue and copper-pink
will be framed
by fir, cedar, and hemlock.

Fishing lines will hum
against blazing muscles
of red flesh.

All these years
river canyon has waited
to sing her true song.

CANYON

I wanted to fish here but there were cliffs,
thorns, wasps, underwater drops
where men drowned.

Two and three-foot leaping chromers,
fresh from the sea,
year after year.

Pine in the air,
and blood on rocks
was fishes' and mine.

Petroglyphs and cliff trails showed
men netted here
thousands of years.

I can say more
but to know
you must go

before melting glaciers
change experiences like these
maybe forever.

NEAR PAISLEY, OREGON

the ancient lake's giant
redband trout
fin small creeks.

Among swirling
ice sculptures
in thawing Chewaucan River,

I daydreamed their lateral lines
as one long red sunset
after a bad storm,

Buddhist monks
pushing children
on swings.

CHINESE DREAM ON THE CANADIAN BORDER

I have two books: the Bible
and Kesey's *Sometimes a Great Notion*,
and the guard says "只有一本书"
translation: "Only one book!"

The language of the Bible
is trees, mountains, rivers,
and can never be destroyed
so, Lord forgive me, I choose Kesey's book.

It's torso river cover
looks like the Siletz in Oregon
where I trolled for sea-run cutts
between the Movie House below Coyote Rock
and my deckhand Tristan's on Siletz Bay.

Maybe I choose the book because
Merry Prankster Kesey
was a Coyote too, of sorts,
a trickster omen,
vanishing in thickets
like his character Hank Stamper who said
"And if Oregon was to get into it
with California I'd fight for Oregon."

Now California, Oregon, and
Washington all speak Chinese,
and I wonder aloud
"How long before Mt. Rushmore
has the face of '黄帝?"
translation: "Yellow Emperor?"
"Already does," says the guard in English.

In Kesey's book there is a disoriented deer
swimming out to sea
like throngs of migrants to Canada,
two languages of man,
visceral and wise,
Heart of the Pacific Northwest
that changes all invaders,
gift and sacrifice and renewal beyond
anyone's wildest dreams

SALAMANDER

paws in tai chi across reed pond
to find a worm or hopper
under cherry blossom clouds,
Pacific Northwest breeze,

joyful eating, mating,
resting in autumn,
unseen by cubicled bodies
in marble towers

or similar cemetery on the hill.

ALBINO DEER IN SNOWSTORM

has red jewel eyes
like holly berries
that trance
powerful as any ritual
killing,

like a virgin
drunk at a college party
asking for anyone
to drive her home.

Later,
there will be a legend
of "Taj Mahal
sold for a nickel,"

mermaid shadow fleeing
truck in icy river,
in the opposite lane
a young couple
with great hope
who didn't stand a chance.

IN OLD GROWTH FOREST

I don't want to see van Gogh, Renoir, Monet,
read Rilke or Kafka, hear Mozart, or anything,
no matter how artful, from a human mind.

Instead, I focus my yarn fly along giant logs,
undercut cliffs, ready for the instant I feel
winter's electric strike.

In hanging moss, creek music, sunlight
through ancient fir and spruce,
beside elk, raccoon, heron tracks in mud

men harvest blazing silver and pink steelhead
fresh from God's ocean.
At night I smile well-rested and joyful

like I slept in a land of Paradise dreams
a thousand years.

MY RIVER

where a leaping spring chinook
startled like a flying saucer,

where I casted with fisher's daughters
innocent as daffodils,

where eagles taloned wriggling silver,
coyote tracks danced in heron feathers.

Where I canoed and waded
in summer current.

Where I caught leaping steelhead,
and poured in my lover's ashes.

Where climate scientists say
may soon be a dry riverbed.

SPAWNING RUN

How many seeds inside a seed?
How far does north go?

I'm on my spawning run north
over I-205 Bridge

and salmon below in the Columbia
are on theirs.

The *Statesman Journal* reports
over 60 degree water is killing them

in Clackamas, Santiam, Willamette Rivers
before they have a chance

and, unless lightning strikes
minds of politicians in Paris,

I wonder how long before we
have lost our chance.

MIRAGE

Ducks expected a pond
but crashed into ice
then all but one recovered
and flew off.

The injured one
spent all night
running back and forth
along shoreline.

By morning, coyote tracks
and carnival of feathers
told the story.

PIGEON

Torn by fishing line, she limped to beach.
"We should save her," I told an old-timer.

"Nah, eagles will eat her by morn," he said.
Morn came and she was still there

staring like a ragged puppy
as I cast under a pier for salmon.

I set my rod down, put her in a box.
Amid smirks and scorns,

drove her to a vet.
A few weeks later when she flew away

it gave me hope against all odds
we can slow a warming climate, rising seas.

COYOTE'S PREDICTION

There is a ghost
like water healing
river's paddle wounds,

old logging mill
lanced by seeds
of forgotten giants,

salmon cannery
weathered like ribs
of a fish skeleton.

Only things
that belong here
will last.

WINTER STEELHEAD

Chrome-bright sword
with steelblue back
leaping
for a visible second,

arcing flame
of Pacific muscle
shaking off
sea lice

letting me know
that while
humans huddle
by wood fires,

snow coats
evergreen forests,
and sun moves
lazy on the horizon,

the ancient spell
of 10, 000 years
is still alive.

EMERGENCE

As a boy, fishing on Whidbey Island,
my reel screamed.

It was likely a giant salmon, orca,
halibut, sea lion or submarine.

When I was nearly spooled,
I jumped in a boat to follow.

It took me across Admiralty Inlet
to Seiku then open sea.

It grew dark and
stars lit the sky.

Whatever it was ran
and ran and ran.

The next morning
I nearly had a glimpse.

I chased it over 30 years,
and I'm still chasing.

ABOUT THE AUTHOR

Scott T. Starbuck was raised fishing rivers near Mt. Hood, in eastern Oregon, and on the Oregon coast. He still dreams swarms of orange salmonfiles gulped by giant redside trout on the Deschutes. After high school, he ran the Tradewinds' *Starfisher* in Depoe Bay.

Later, he was a 2013 Artsmith Fellow on Orcas Island, 2014 Friends of William Stafford Scholar at the "Speak Truth to Power" Fellowship of Reconciliation Seabeck Conference, and a writer-in-residence at The Sitka Center for Art and Ecology, just inshore from where he fished for salmon, halibut, lingcod, and rockfish eight years.

Now he serves as a Co-Creative Writing Coordinator at San Diego Mesa College, and writes an ecopoetry / fishing blog *Trees, Fish, and Dreams* at riverseek.blogspot.com

Starbuck's fine art book of fishing poems *River Walker* (Mountains and Rivers, 2012) sold out of it's small press printing of 200 copies in about a year. Based on his love for salmon and salmon people, he wrote The City of Depoe Bay's Memorial Against Offshore Oil Drilling to the Oregon Governor's Ocean Resources Management Task Force in 1989 to help stop oil rigs off the Oregon Coast. He was awarded a second PLAYA residency in July 2016 to work alongside climate scientists or science writers, artists, and authors as he develops his third book of ecopoems *Chewaucan Wars*.

He said "During spring, summer, and winter breaks from teaching, I spend more time with my fishing rod than I do with people." His fishing articles or poems appeared in *Yale Anglers' Journal, Salmon Trout Steelheader, The Sunday Oregonian, Northwest Fishing Reports, Talking River* at Lewis-Clark State College, *The Raven Chronicles*, and many other literary journals.

www.ingramcontent.com/pod-product-compliance
Lightning Source LLC
Chambersburg PA
CBHW031158020426
42333CB00013B/718